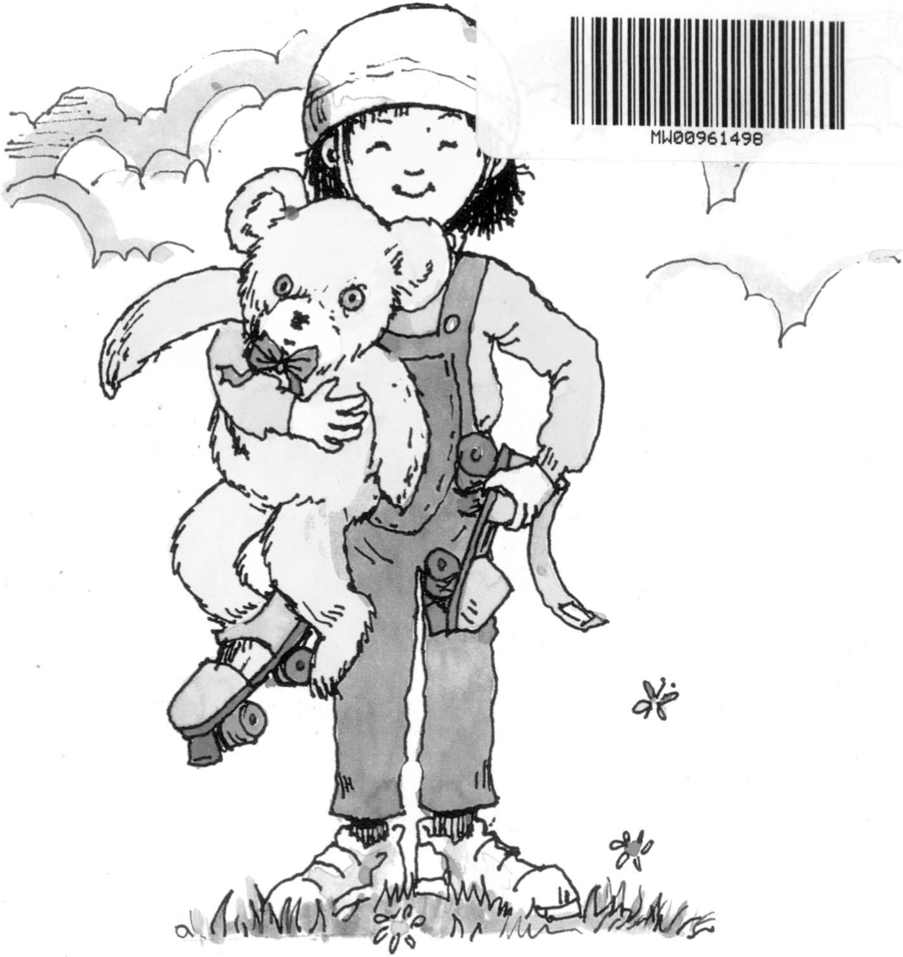

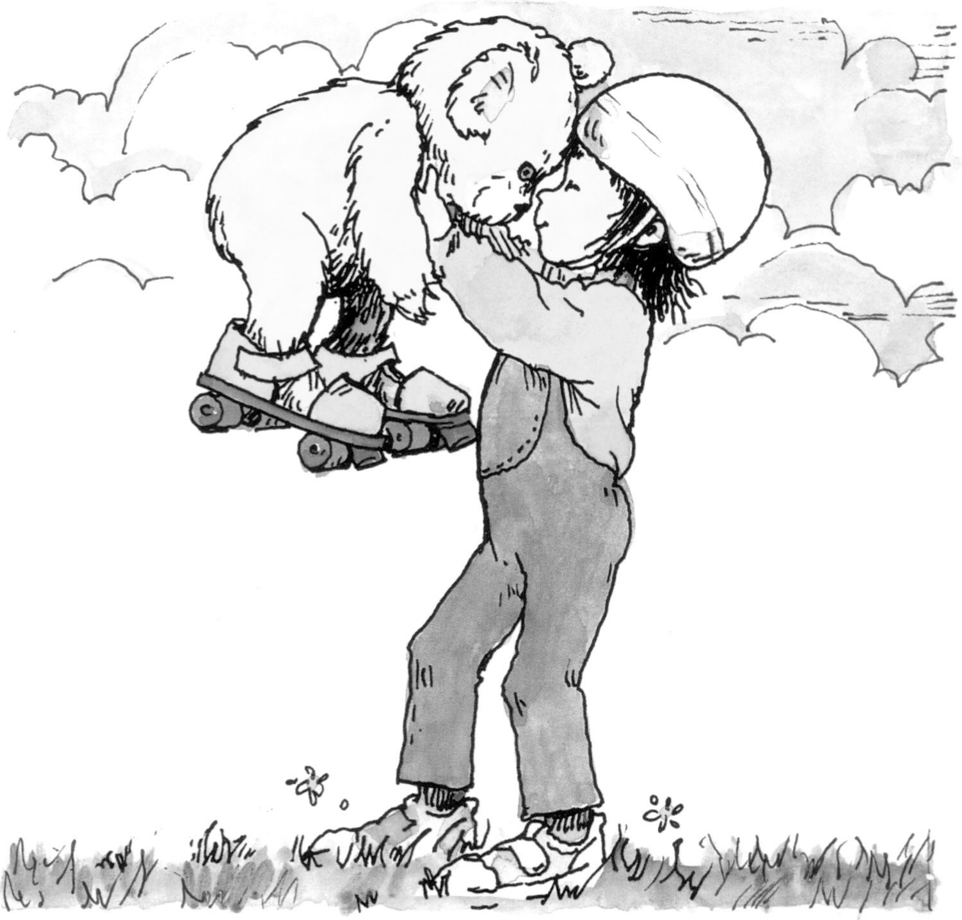

You can skate

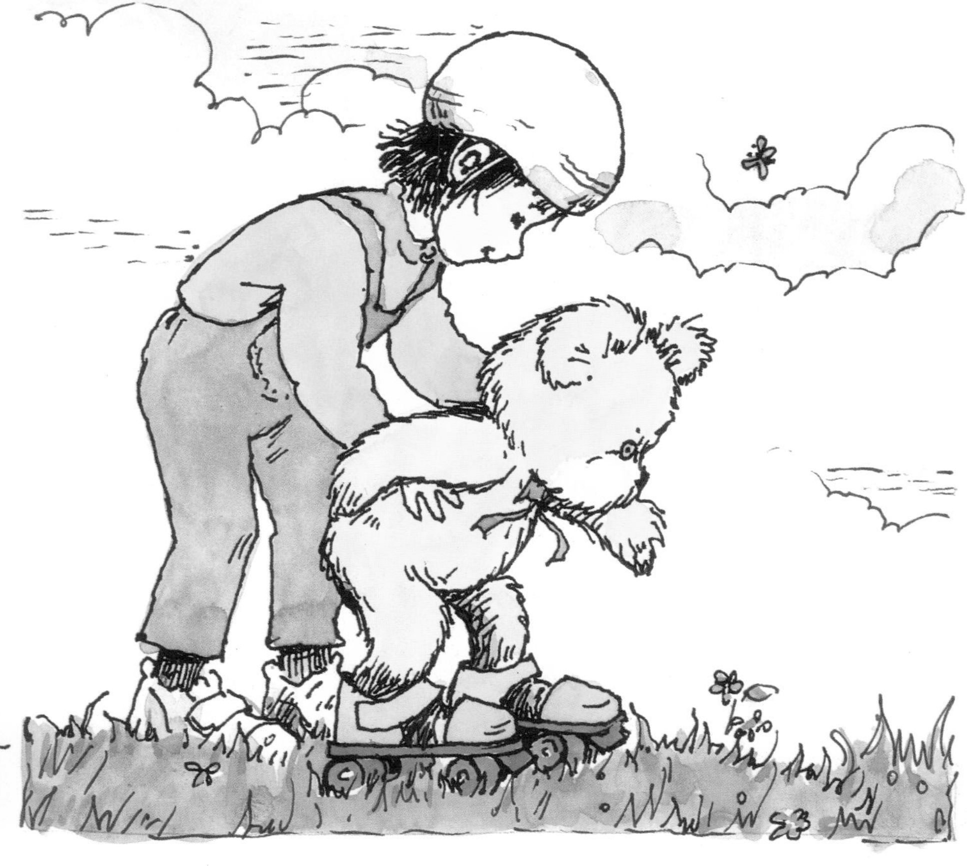

on the grass.

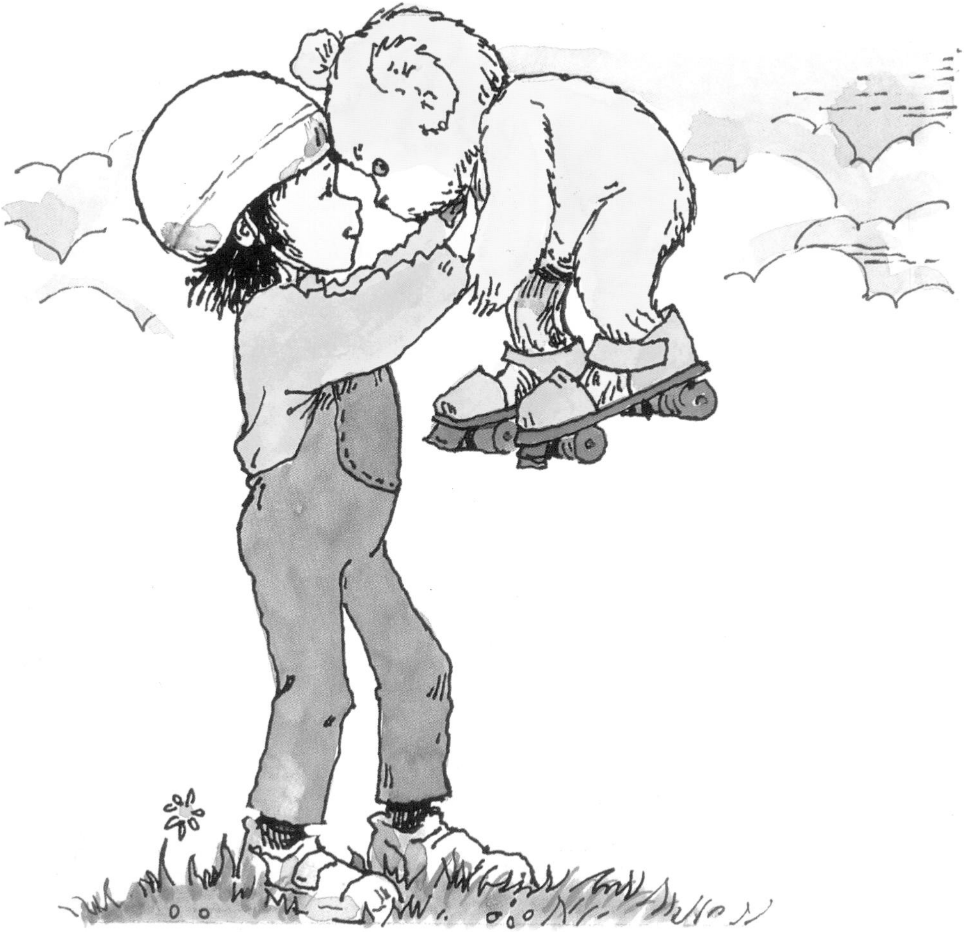

You can skate

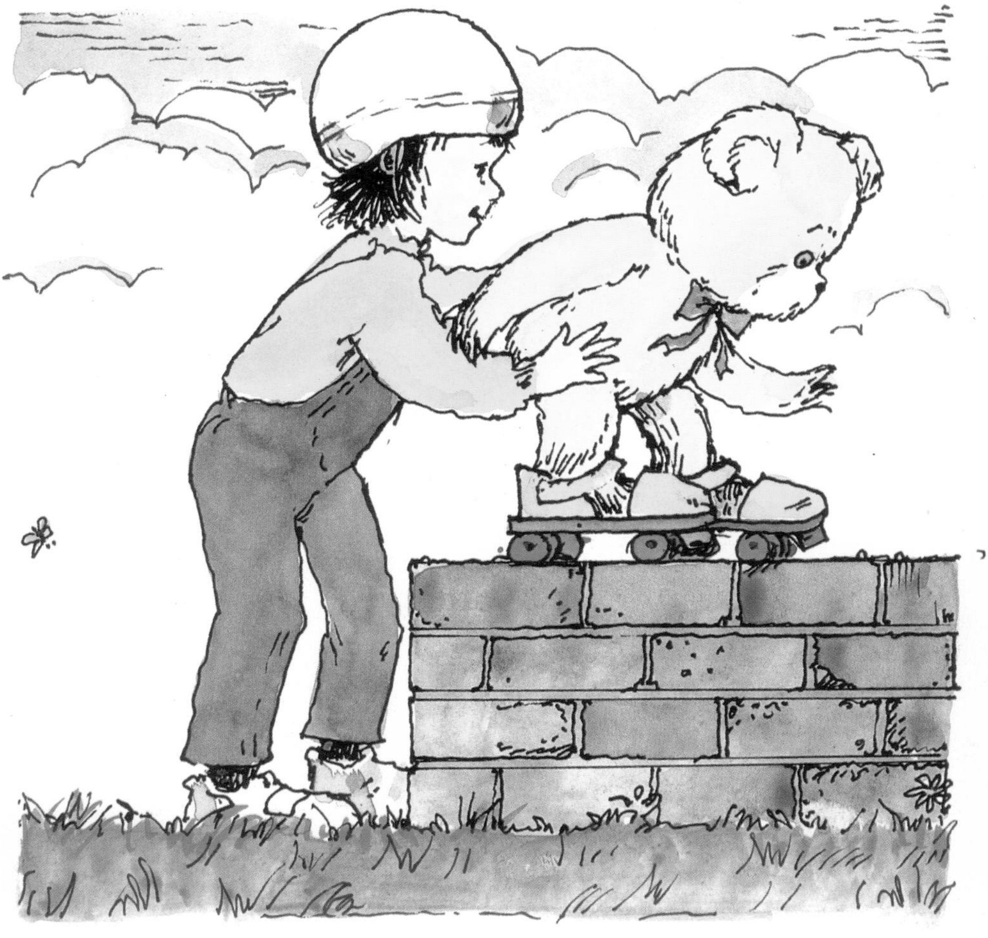

on the wall.

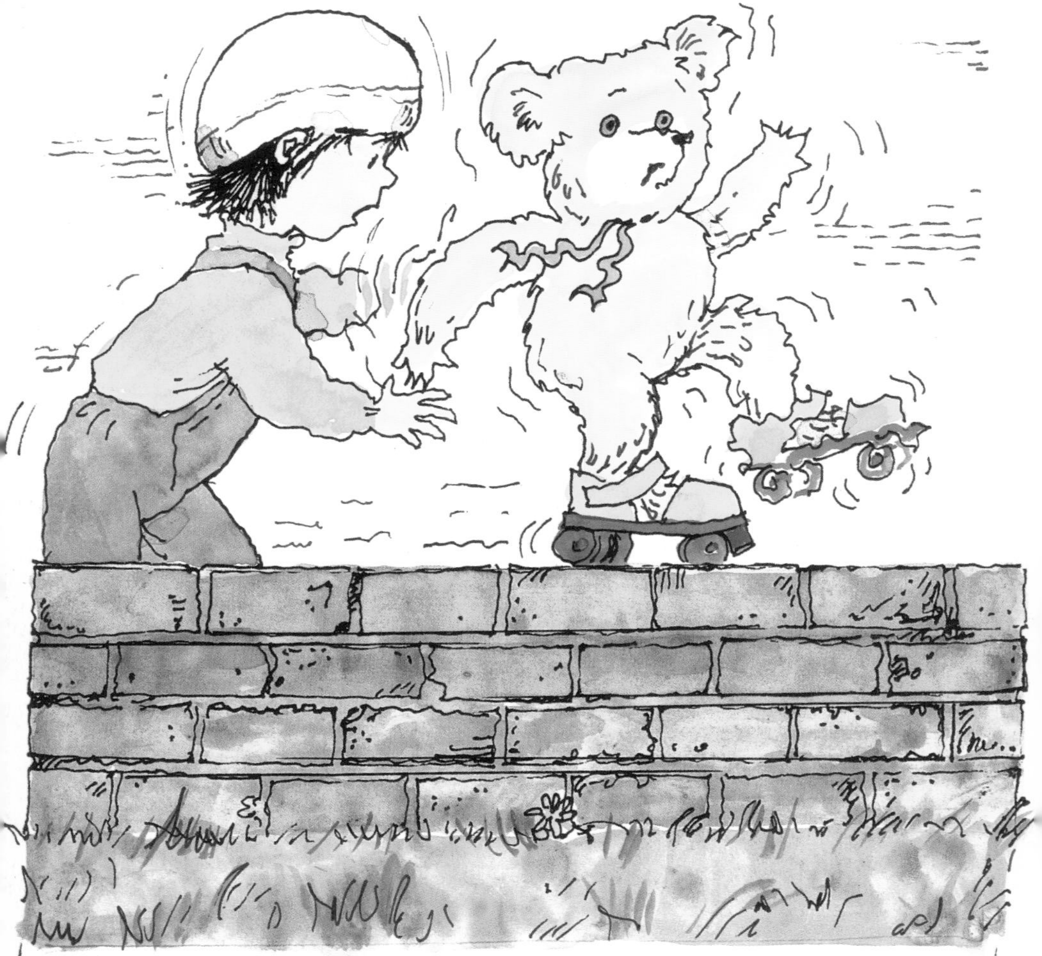

Oh no!

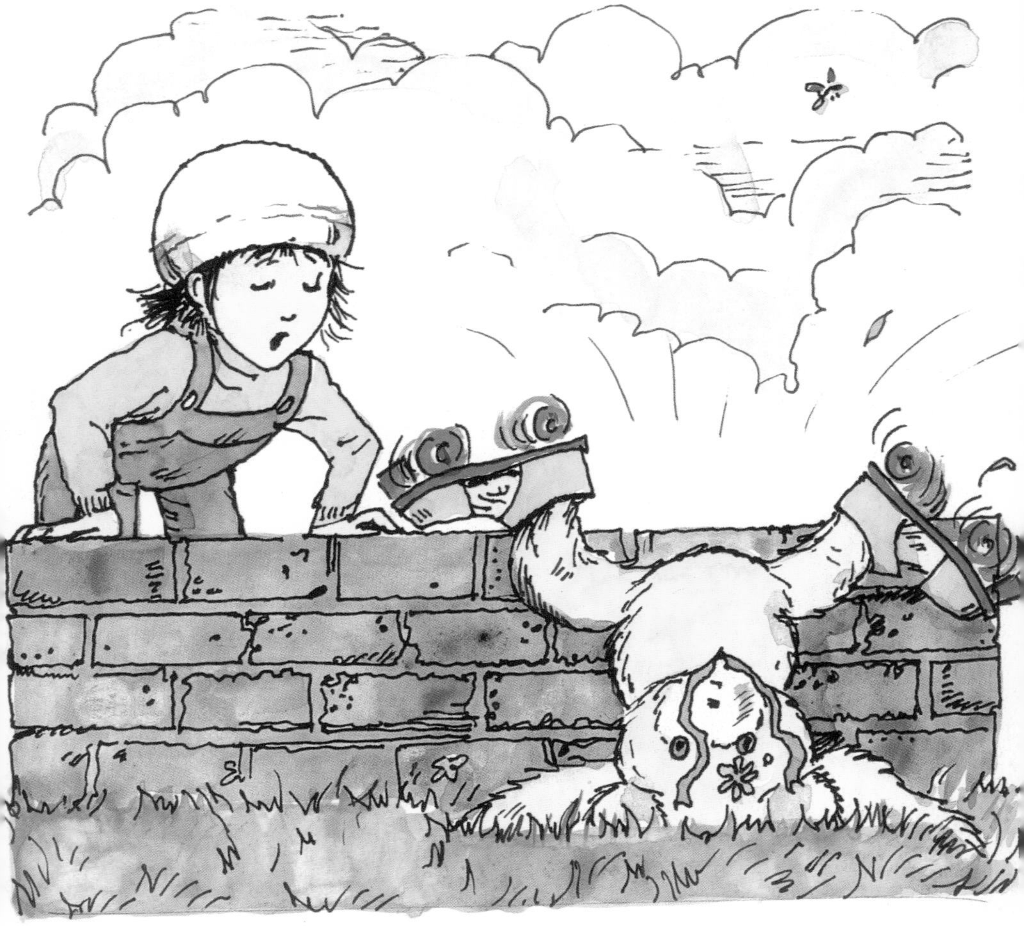

Crash!

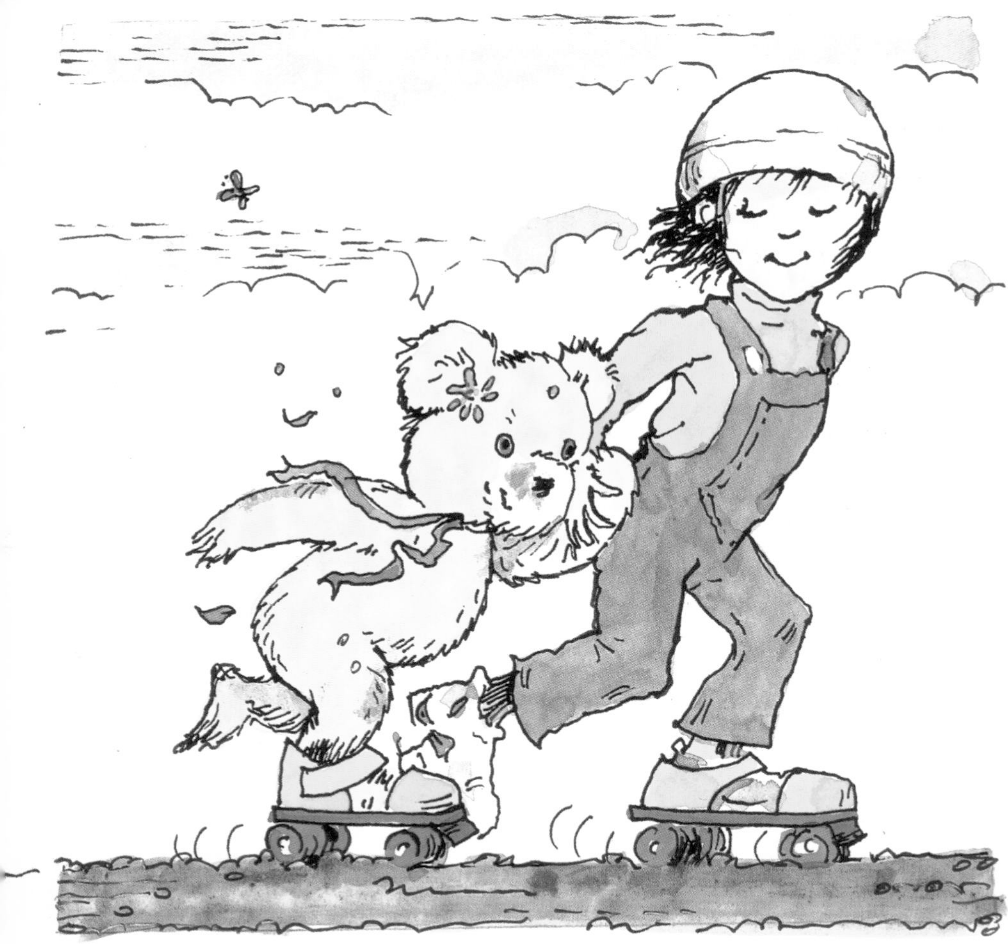

Skate with me.